All of the Ocean

Louise Alexandra Erskine

Better isn't always higher Sometimes it's deeper

This book isn't quite like the others on your shelf, it wants you to write in it, it wants you to make notes in the margins happy ones, sad ones, angry ones, wherever the wind blows you its your book write what you feel. Use the prompt suggestions and add your thoughts or feelings. Add ideas for your own poems or stories whatever you do don't leave it blank, it wants you to doodle in it to illustrate the poems and dog ear the pages. This book doesn't mind if you drip coffee or leave fingerprints and ink smudges. This book doesn't want to be just a book it wants to be a friend.

Thalassophile

(n.) A lover of the Sea or Ocean.

For all the wild ocean people trying to tame themselves for a world they don't feel they fit, for Stephanie who showed me the power in my voice, for the people who believed in me and - and gave me someone to prove right instead of wrong, and for T who looked at me with wonder and whose own soul held up a mirror that showed me how much I carry and the difference I can make.

The ocean is still the ocean
whether it kisses the shoreline or not
the moon
does not fall from the sky
simply because it is time for the sun to shine
a mountain rises
magnificent from the dust
whether anyone is climbing it or not
I do not stop being me
an insatiable, inspired, beautiful
mix of darkness and starlight
just because
someone that should have loved me
did not.

It'll take an entire
ocean of tears
to miss you
just a little less
and even that wont be enough
to dilute the love.

You're an ocean
full of life, beauty and wonder
so why do you stay here
at the shoreline
trying to fit all that
unfathomable depth
into such a tiny bucket
hoping to be carried home
by someone you know
is just going to empty
you back out
before they leave.

~ Empty buckets

He kissed me
like I was oxygen
and he was
drowning.

Safe
in your harbour
I forgot
a ship belongs
on the ocean.

It's not that this isn't fun
jumping in puddles
splashing about on the surface
but you're an entire ocean
and I want to dive deeper
where the light
finds it harder to shine.

For all the people
who looked at the darkness
in you and were scared
I hope you know
all I ever saw was
the stars.

Your kisses on my neck
fingers trailing
slowly across my ribcage
you and I
rising together with the sun.

Tethered at your shoreline
I walk along the sand
wondering what it is
I'm still holding on to
when I know I'll never swim.

~ Letting go of you again

It seems to me
we have a choice
each of us to make
to either stand here
longing for distant shores
or to set about
building the boat
that will take us to them.

~ Building starts with you.

At the end of the day
I just want someone
whose darkness fits
with my darkness
and whose light
causes mine to shine
a little brighter.

This life crushes
each of us
at one time or another
and sometimes
all there is to do
is trust in the process
believing that the wave
knows when to break.

Bathic

(adj.) Pertaining to depth especially of the sea.

Turbulent

Write a lyric/micro/poem/thought/short story/ journal entry/basically whatever you want even a doodle using the above prompt for inspiration.

She spent every day
trying to keep above water
just to loose herself
to the flood every night.

~ We don't have to wear our masks in the
dark.

She felt his love
like she felt the weather
and always knew
when a storm was coming.

There was always
going to be
one hell of a storm
but my God
the lightning we made
was spectacular.

How strange it is to
trawl the ocean for a fish
having tethered my soul
to the Kraken.

~ When they say "there's plenty more fish in
the sea".

More than Starlight

Sometimes
just breathing
can leave you feeling
crushed and not revived
like you're an ocean
stripped of all its salt
and wondering
am I not now a lake instead
or a mountain
beginning to crumble
asking yourself how far
do I have to fall
before I become a foothill
how many knocks can you take
before you wonder
is it even worth it
before you ask yourself
what it is you're even fighting for
but know this
the fire isn't burning you
its refining you
and if it were easy
you wouldn't know

just how much you could overcome
you wouldn't know
how much grit you had
and you would have carried on
sailing through life
thinking its okay just to be
a light in the dark
without ever realising
you were an entire galaxy
full of stars.

~ You're more than you know.

Reaching for the surface
the weight of this loneliness
dragging me back under
as my heart aches for you.

I can let this moment wash over me
let it drown me
choke me beneath the waves
or I can take it
and let it teach me how to swim.

She was powerless
standing
in the face of the storm
so she simply surrendered
watched it roll on in
and loved him till
it passed.

I didn't see it at the time
I was too lost inside the storm
but you were my lighthouse
illuminating those
thundering skies
keeping me safe
& leading me home.

Mångata

(n.) The reflection of the moon on the water.

Undercurrent

Write a lyric/micro/poem/thought/short story/
journal entry/basically whatever you want even a
doodle using the above prompt for inspiration.

I can handle being wrong
I can handle failure
I can fall down
and I can pick myself back up
what I can't handle is being stuck
so even if its just
one tiny tip toe
step at a time
I have to put one foot
in-front of the other
because like a shark
that can't stop swimming
I have to be moving forwards.

Would you take a shot
on one last roll of the dice
to feel that
lightning strike kind of love
only our stormy souls
can make.

I would have drown
smiling if it was in your
ocean.

It had Taken her many years
she had built the walls
tall and strong
but for him
she was able to put in a door
and when she opened it
she found that she could
see the sea.

Can you imagine the chaos
if the north star declined to shine
incase the other stars
were feeling insecure
or imagine the turmoil
if each wave held itself back
fearing rejection from the shore
imagine that the wind
thought itself above
sweeping the leaves up as it blows
or the nightingale stayed silent
to timid to be heard
imagine what life would look like
if the earth refused to turn
or if you realised
you were all you needed
and you let your fire burn.

~ It's time to stop listening to the opinions of
people that haven't earned the right to share them.

She didn't know what it was
but she felt it in her dreams
and when she awoke
it was as though
the sea was calling to her.

Theres beauty to be found
in that space between
asking the questions
and finding the answers
in the healing
between the wound and the scar
in the time
the ocean waves are swelling
but have yet to
break upon the shore.

Not even all this darkness
I've been carrying
for all this time I've
been carrying it
is enough to eclipse
the light you shine
as you illuminate
all the wonder i carry inside
that life had taught
my heart it was supposed to hide.

You are all of the ocean
and I'm just sat here
on the shore
trying to figure out
how to wrap my heart
around you.

He was my ocean
I was his moon
and together
we changed the tide.

There will always be those
mornings of magic
where we see the moon
standing beside the sun
reminding us
we are more powerful
when we rise together.

When they met
her heart was locked tight
and she was afraid
but she threw the key
into the waves
for to her
he was the sea.

Sonder

(n.) The realisation that each passer by has a life as vivid and complex as your own.

Ocean

_____

_____

_____

_____

_____

_____

_____

_____

_____

_____

_____

_____

_____

_____

_____

_____

_____

_____

_____

_____

Write a lyric/micro/poem/thought/short story/
journal entry/basically whatever you want even a
doodle using the above prompt for inspiration.

I stood at the edge
of your shoreline
watching the tide recede
until there came a point
where the ocean
no longer kissed my feet
and I waved goodbye
as I finally put to bed
the possibility
of you and me.

~ Letting go.

The waves were high
and she was adrift
but she wasn't afraid
for to her
he was the sea.

I want to be
the sky above
your ocean.

You & I
we may share
the same darkness
but baby
we know how to
light up
the entire sky.

And then there was
that moment
the whole world slipped away
into slow motion
and there was nothing
but you and me
and your eyes
and I could get lost in them forever
completely found.

What if not just every heartbreak
but every triumph
all life's trials and all it's lessons
and each and every moment
that I'm built of
has been leading me to you
what if every rise and every fall
of every wave that pushed me forward
did so because it knew
that in the end the only shore
my ship ever really needed to crash into
was the one that belonged to you.

You will forever
be my Ocean.

There's treasure and gold
and the bones of men
who's tales will never be told
hidden amidst the
shipwrecks and broken dreams
of you and me
and the things that we could never be
as they lay lost and forgotten
forging lonely homes
for creatures lurking in the deep
comforted as they hide
amongst the broken pieces
of a love that will forever scatter
the desolate ocean floor.

Oh don't mind me
I'll just be over here
loving you
trying not to drown
in the depth of it.

There's a certain
kind of sweetness
to the anticipation
of setting out
and sailing
into uncharted waters
trusting you
to take me deeper
than I could ever swim alone.

You and I we take the train
into the city or out to the coast
just to be
somewhere else
standing in our favourite coats
eating chips
trying to escape the waves
as they catch
and soak our feet
sneaking into bars
kissing in the back seat
of someone else's car
in trouble again for talking
passing notes instead
when we were fifteen and thinking
we knew what love should be
believing every single moment
would feel just like it did
sitting close together
on the back seat of the bus
smiling as we're strumming on
your beat up old guitar
when you were looking in my eyes
and singing oh-oh la-la.

Kiss my neck and
leave me breathless
warm lips on bare skin
as we tumble into
one another
like the waves upon the shore.

Numinous

(adj.) Feeling both fearful and awed by what is before you.

Tide

_____

_____

_____

_____

_____

_____

_____

_____

_____

_____

_____

_____

_____

_____

_____

_____

_____

_____

Write a lyric/micro/poem/thought/short story/
journal entry/basically whatever you want even a
doodle using the above prompt for inspiration.

Through all of this
I hope you know
I see you
golden sands
sun shining
buried treasure
I'm longing to hold
and I know you see me
out here
and that it might be difficult
to understand
as you watch me turn away
and sail into yet another storm
instead of continuing toward you
but the truth is
I need to become a better sailor
before I can settle
on your shore.

I was a hell of a sailor
but his
was no ordinary storm
and in a love
that should have been
my anchor
the waves threw me off course.

Meet me at the shoreline
let the waves kiss our feet
take me by the hand
and lead me
my naked soul
cleansed in the water with you.

You be the sea you me
& I'll be the sky for you.

~ Even if it's just for tonight.

He rolled over me
like a storm
before I'd battened down
the hatches
but I went down
with that ship smiling.

And it was when
we had each
stopped our hearts
from searching
that love
was able to find us
the way the ocean
finds the shore.

There's so much more to you
than everyone gets to see
like pirate gold
concealed beneath layers of spice
treasure hiding in plain sight
until we're alone and suddenly
in all the places
I used to be the lock
with you I become the key
something happens
when were together
embers don't just spark they ignite
it's been a long time
since I believed in fairytales
but right now looking in your eyes
it feels like maybe
you were made for me.

Here I am holding out
like a castle on the sand
knowing the tide is coming
and waiting
for the crash of the wave
that will finally allow my surrender
to the oceans pull.

She was the storm
raging across the ocean
until she crashed into his shore
tell me
have you ever seen what happens
when the lightning
strikes the sand.

There have been
too many days
I've felt
like a wave
tossed on the ocean
so out of control
the current
pulling one way
as the wind
is pushing another
and I'm just
caught in the middle
desperately fighting
not to get lost
in somebody else's storm.

Broken boat blessings

We invest so much of ourselves
searching for someone
to sail with
off into the sunset
but what happens once
we have them
when we think the search is over
then we find ourselves
drifting out
into a sea that's much too deep
before we discover
that the sails contain
a few unexpected tears
before we realise that
the decks were only polished
to cover up the scars
and now
there are splinters beneath our feet
what happens when we realise
the ship is sitting in the water
just a little bit too low
trying to carry a load that's far to heavy
or that the time wasn't taken

to properly fix the leaks
and now
that those patches
are wearing through
there's no way
to keep the water out
what if the ship doesn't
have the crew you thought
what if
it's really run by pirates
and they're just gunning
for your treasure
the truth is I don't know
I can't answer any of that
What I do know is
the blessing
is often in the broken
but not everyone is brave enough
to see it
And even if you are
there's still a choice to make
and it isn't one that's easy
do you stay and fix something
that you didn't break
or to climb into a lifeboat alone

accepting
you can't force
someone else to heal
and if you do leave what then
how do you let go
how do you let go
of the disappointment
or harder still the hope
but still hold on enough to pray
that maybe if it's right
some day
you'll climb aboard again
and what if
by the time it comes
your soul is just too tired
because it isn't easy
to keep on looking out
into the unknown
when you only ever seem to
row against the tide
and no one ever
even showed you how
and all we can do
any one of us
before we each set sail

is to make sure
we know that we can swim
so when the waters
get too choppy
or the boat
breaks upon the rocks
we have a hope
we can hold on to
that we won't ever
truly drown.

Acatalepsy

(n.) The impossibility to truly comprehend anything.

Billow

Write a lyric/micro/poem/thought/short story/ journal entry/basically whatever you want even a doodle using the above prompt for inspiration.

We made a wreck
of the ship
we were trying to build
long before
we even lost sight
of the shore.

All I'm asking
is that
you take a breath
and step into the
unfathomable depth
of my reckless love.

You can rage against me
with your storms
hurl your waves upon my deck
throw lightning bolts
surge the tides
and toss the winds to blow me down
I know your able
to summon the leviathan from the depths
and command the kraken
with just a look
but even now
with my torn up sails
and broken mast
I am the captain of this ship
and the more storms I weather
the more greatness I carry
as I sail into destiny
and you watch on
realising
you're caught in a storm you created
with nothing but a rowboat
to cling too.

She was alone
lost out to sea
& broken by the storm
but as each wave battered her
it bought her
closer to the shore.

I don't know about you
but I'm ready to stop running
to stop wishing on stars
& fitting my dreams in somebody
else's back pocket
I'm ready to stop taking
the fight to the dragon
& letting him lay waste to me
in a breath
ready to stop slaying the kraken
I'll leave him to the depths
I'm done crashing into the waves
and letting the riptide pull me under
I don't know about you
but I'm ready to stop
chasing tornadoes
& just surrender to the infinite
possibility of limitless love.

And all her broken pieces
longed for the
ocean waves
not to wash them away
but to let them flow
together.

The thing I am holding
close to my heart
is that
somewhere out there
you're under the same sky.

Maybe the miracle
isn't the waters parting
maybe its you becoming
a strong enough swimmer
to keep your head
above the waves
when they don't.

Sometimes
as I stand here in the dark
I feel that I too
am like the waning moon
heart full of craters
half cloaked
with mystery and i'll admit
a little darkness
as I wait here
for your axis to turn
until finally
you see me
shining beautifully
in all my fullness.

Take me beyond
the breakwater
let me dive beneath
the surface
and swim through
your ocean until
exhausted
I wash upon the sand.

Fall into my eyes
break beneath the surface
dive where the
waters still run deep.

There are times
in which I fear
you and I are destined
only ever to occupy
that space
where candy floss clouds
bleed into indigo waves
as sunsets fall
into oceans deep
always in sight
never in reach
forever trapped
at our own horizon.

Yūgen

(n.) A profound, mysterious sense of the beauty of the universe that triggers a deep emotional response.

Riptide

_____

_____

_____

_____

_____

_____

_____

_____

_____

_____

_____

_____

_____

_____

_____

_____

_____

_____

_____

Write an epigram/micro/poem/thought/short story/
journal entry/basically whatever you want even a
doodle using the above prompt for inspiration.

The sea
the sky
the way my heart feels
when you are near
some things
are to beautiful
to be destroyed
with understanding.

As he looked at her
and their eyes met
her troubles fell into the sea.

She often marvelled
at how he could anchor her
without weighing her down.

There are two ways to
survive a storm
batten down the hatches
remain beneath
and wait for it to pass
or
rise above it
where the skies are clear.

A fire that burns
the way ours does
is a terrifying thing
to keep into.

On the stormy days

When the world is spinning
and its just a little bit to fast
when the wind is howling
and the waves are crashing all around
when you're alone in so much darkness
you can't even see the stars
I'll be with you in the battles
and in the dreams that feel just a little bit too far

When it feels as though you're drowning
and the sky is out of reach
when your strength seems to be failing
and you just can't fight the tide
when you're facing down a struggle
you don't even understand
I'll be in the boat beside you
and the two of us together will make it to the sand

When you're feeling like a cause that's lost
and it seems there's no way out
when your operating from a deficit
and the world weighs more than you can bear
when you feel that life is stacked against you

and you're not playing with a deck that's full
Ill stay here fighting in your corner
all for one and one for all

When there are days you fall like lightning
and you're laying in the dirt
when the current pulls you far from shore
and you're needing to feel seen
when you fail to see you're beautiful
or that it's through each and every scar
Ill be right here beside you
gently reminding you who you are

When every struggle that you face
Leaves you feeling like a mistake
when you aren't sure if you'll endure it
or if the change is worth the pain
when life does its best to derail you
through every victory & not just in the loss
I hope you know that I rejoice in how you started
and that this journey is worth the cost

When the cameras get put down no-ones watching
and there's not a smile left to fake
when your experience diminishes your expectation

and you can't seem to find your hope
when you're doubting you're own decisions
and all the things you think and feel
I'll gladly walk each pathway that you've chosen
believing in the dream you're so bravely daring to
make real.

Selcouth

(adj.) Something unfamiliar, unusual or wondrous.

Fathom

Write an epigram/micro/poem/thought/short story/
journal entry/basically whatever you want even a
doodle using the above prompt for inspiration

A SINGLE DROP OF THE OCEAN

for mixed choir a cappella

LOUISE ALEXANDRA

HENRIK DAHLGREN

2

103

4

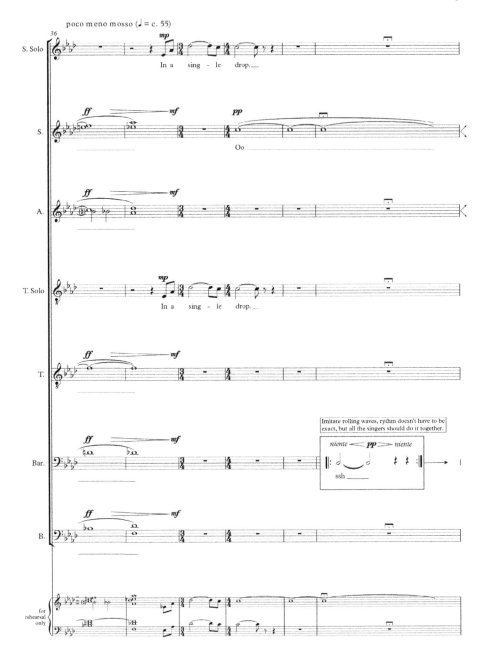

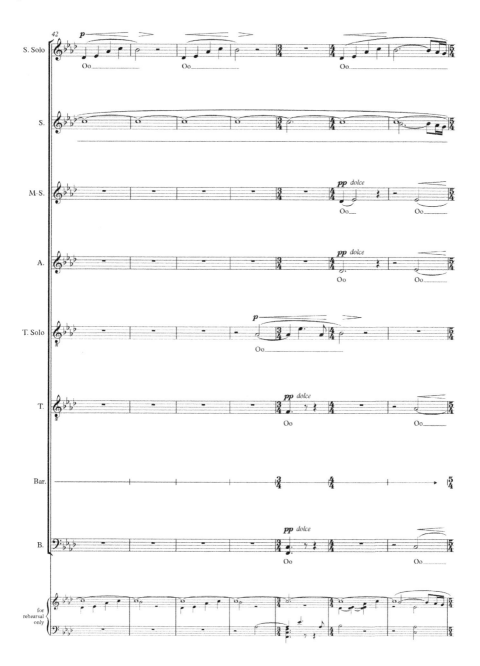

Repeat 3-5 times, poco a poco diminuendo

tempo primo (♩ = c. 60)

A Single Drop of the Ocean

Musical composition - Henrik Dahlgen
Instagram @henkeestelle
Lyrics - Louise Alexandra Erskine
Instagram @ beautifully_defected

To all the ocean people that made it this far, my prayer for this book has always been that it would find its way into the hands that needed to hold it. I don't know how life bought you to this point, to this time, place or stage of crushing but I do know that whatever you've been through, however you got here you are the answer to that prayer. My hope now is that even if it was just through one poem something in this book bought you the comfort, healing or inspiration that you needed and let you know that you are never truly alone in what you endure. My prayer now is that if tears were shed that they bought you closer to that place of peace we all search for, and that in doing so it extends a ripple effect of grace and compassion outward to those around you. No matter what happens going forward I hope you remember you weren't designed to fit inside anyone else's bucket.

~ parting words.

Notes

Notes

Notes

Notes

Notes

Notes

Notes

Notes

Index

Printed in Great Britain
by Amazon

79881297R00072